IMAGES
of America

PRESIDIO OF
MONTEREY

This is a photograph from the early 1960s, taken from the Fort Mervine ramparts on the Presidio of Monterey, showing the Sloat Monument on the left and overlooking the beautiful Monterey Bay.

IMAGES
of America

PRESIDIO OF
MONTEREY

Harold E. Raugh, Jr.

ARCADIA

Published by Arcadia Publishing
Charleston SC, Chicago IL, Portsmouth NH, San Francisco CA

Printed in Great Britain

Library of Congress Catalog Card Number: 2003116178

For all general information contact Arcadia Publishing at:
Telephone 843-853-2070
Fax 843-853-0044
E-mail sales@arcadiapublishing.com
For customer service and orders:
Toll-Free 1-888-313-2665

Visit us on the internet at http://www.arcadiapublishing.com

This pre–World War II postcard shows an aerial view of the Monterey Peninsula and Monterey
Bay area, considered by many to be one of the most beautiful places in the United States. The
Presidio of Monterey is shown in the left center of the photograph, the green swath running
generally horizontally and bordered by red-roofed Army barracks and other military buildings.

CONTENTS

ACKNOWLEDGMENTS

The modern Presidio of Monterey, on the California coast overlooking the Pacific Ocean, is a small U.S. military installation that has made significant contributions to our national defense over the last century. The photographs in this book will hopefully show the evolution of the modern Presidio of Monterey as a military installation, as well as a glimpse of the human side of soldiering and of foreign language training in the 20th century and beyond.

Many of the photographs in this book are from the Historical Documents Collection (Archives) of the Defense Language Institute Foreign Language Center and Presidio of Monterey (DLIFLC & POM). I appreciatively acknowledge permission to reproduce these photographs here. I am also grateful for the assistance of Joseph Morgan; Sgt. Maj. Bob Britton, U.S. Army (Ret.); and Wilfred K. Houle in completing this volume.

I am pleased to acknowledge the encouragement and support of Col. Michael R. Simone, commandant of the Defense Language Institute Foreign Language Center and commander of the Presidio of Monterey, in completing this pictorial history and an earlier volume on Fort Ord. Under his leadership, the Defense Language Institute Foreign Language Center—the United States Department of Defense's acknowledged leader in foreign language training—continues to evolve, set precedents, and contribute to our national security.

I hope to be able, through the publication of this book, to help preserve the military history and heritage of the Presidio of Monterey, from its days as an infantry and cavalry post, to its modern incarnation as the home of the Defense Language Institute Foreign Language Center.

—Harold E. Raugh, Jr.

INTRODUCTION

The current Presidio of Monterey is named after the fort ("presidio") and mission established by Capt. Don Gaspar de Portola near Lake El Estero in Monterey after the Spanish officially took possession of Alta California on June 3, 1770. It was originally called El Presidio Royal de Monte Rey. Since that time, on different sites, the Presidio of Monterey has been under the control of Spain (1770 to 1822), Mexico (1822 to 1846), and the United States (since 1846).

After a "premature" attempt by the United States to capture Monterey in 1842, the U.S. Congress declared war on Mexico on May 12, 1846. On July 7, 1846, Commodore John Drake Sloat, then commander of the U.S Pacific Squadron, landed marines and sailors under Capt. William Mervine at Monterey and took possession of California.

The Americans, as soon as they seized Monterey, began building a more effective fortification to protect the anchorage and the town. Construction began on a site uphill from El Castillo, a small artillery battery first built by the Spanish in 1792 to protect the original Presidio. The Americans built a square-shaped stockade encircled with a trench and positioned three 42-pounder cannons on the redoubt. This battery was originally called Fort Stockton, after Commodore Robert F. Stockton, who replaced Sloat in July 1846, then Fort Mervine, after Captain Mervine, who had commanded the first American landing party.

Company F, 3rd Artillery Regiment arrived in Monterey in January 1847, and the U.S. Army then assumed from the Navy responsibility for the continuing construction of Fort Mervine. Two of the artillery lieutenants, William Tecumseh Sherman and E.O.C. Ord, plus Engineer Lt. Henry W. Halleck, were destined to become prominent general officers during the Civil War.

During its early history, this fortification seemed to have many names, including Fort Halleck, Fort Savannah, and the Monterey Redoubt. In 1852, the Monterey Redoubt was renamed the Monterey Ordnance Depot and used until 1856 as a military storehouse. From 1856 until the closing months of the Civil War, the fort (which was then called Ord Barracks) was abandoned. It was manned again in 1865, then abandoned a second time in 1866, although the U.S. government "reserved" for possible future use a 140-acre military reservation surrounding the redoubt.

Near the end of the Philippine Insurrection in 1902, the Army recognized it needed additional forts, particularly on the West Coast. As possible sites were being surveyed, the Army "discovered" that it already owned a large area in Monterey that would be suitable for a military post. In July 1902, the Army announced plans to build a cantonment area and station one infantry regiment at Monterey. The 15th Infantry Regiment—which had fought in China and the Philippines—arrived in Monterey in September 1902 and began building the cantonment area. The 1st Squadron, 9th Cavalry, "Buffalo Soldiers," arrived shortly thereafter.

In 1902, the name of the cantonment area was the Monterey Military Reservation. It was changed to Ord Barracks on July 13, 1903, and to the Presidio of Monterey (POM) on August 30, 1904. Various infantry regiments rotated to the Presidio of Monterey, including the 15th Infantry (1902 to 1906), 20th Infantry (1906 to 1909), and 12th Infantry (1909 to 1917), frequently with supporting cavalry and artillery elements. The Army School of Musketry, the forerunner of the Infantry School, operated at the Presidio of Monterey from 1907 to 1913. In 1917, the U.S. War Department purchased a nearby parcel of 15,609.5 acres of land, called the Gigling Reservation, to use as training areas for Presidio of Monterey troops. This post, supplemented by additional acreage, was renamed Fort Ord on August 15, 1940.

The 11th Cavalry Regiment was posted at the Presidio from 1919 to 1940, and the 2nd Battalion, 76th Field Artillery Regiment, from 1922 to 1940. During the summer months, Presidio soldiers organized and led Civilian Conservation Corps (CCC), Citizens' Military Training Corps (CMTC), and Reserve Officer Training Corps (ROTC) camps in the local area.

In 1940, the Presidio became the temporary headquarters of the III Corps, and served as a reception center until 1944. Declared inactive in late 1944, the Presidio was reopened in 1945 and served as a Civil Affairs Staging and Holding Area (CASA) for civil affairs soldiers preparing for the occupation of Japan.

On November 1, 1941, the Army established the Fourth U.S. Army Intelligence School at the Presidio of San Francisco to teach the Japanese language to Japanese-American (Nisei) soldiers to use in a possible conflict with Japan. War broke out in December 1941, and in 1942 the school was relocated to Minnesota and renamed the Military Intelligence Service Language School (MISLS)

In 1946, after World War II, the MISLS was moved to the Presidio of Monterey. It added Russian, Chinese, Korean, Arabic, and six other languages to its curriculum. It was renamed the Army Language School (ALS) in 1947. The size of the faculty and student classes, and number of languages taught, increased throughout the Cold War years of the 1950s and later.

A number of service language schools were combined in 1963, when the ALS was redesignated the Defense Language Institute, West Coast Branch (DLIWC), with its headquarters in Washington, D.C. In 1974, the DLI headquarters moved to the Presidio of Monterey. After all service language training was consolidated, the DLI was renamed the Defense Language Institute Foreign Language Center (DLIFLC) in 1976.

DLIFLC was granted academic accreditation in 1978 and expanded in the 1980s. Instructor-to-student ratios increased, and with the introduction of advanced teaching techniques and information-age technology, average student language proficiency steadily increased.

For many years, DLIFLC was a tenant activity on the Presidio of Monterey, and the Presidio was a sub-installation of the nearby Fort Ord. Fort Ord closed in 1994, and the Presidio of Monterey again became a separate installation, the DLIFLC and POM.

The DLIFLC continues to evolve and expand its language course offerings in the wake of the end of the Cold War and to support the Global War on Terrorism. Currently training more than 3,000 resident students in more than 75 languages and dialects yearly, the DLIFLC is the premier foreign language training institution in the world.

One

1902–1918

THE MODERN PRESIDIO
OF MONTEREY

The 15th Infantry Regiment, fresh from combat service in China and the Philippines, arrived in 1902 to construct the "modern" Monterey Military Reservation (the name was changed to Ord Barracks in 1903 and to the Presidio of Monterey in 1904). The soldiers cleared an area and established a tent encampment that was used until barracks were built and occupied the following year. The site of the original 1902–1903 tent encampment is now called "Soldier Field."

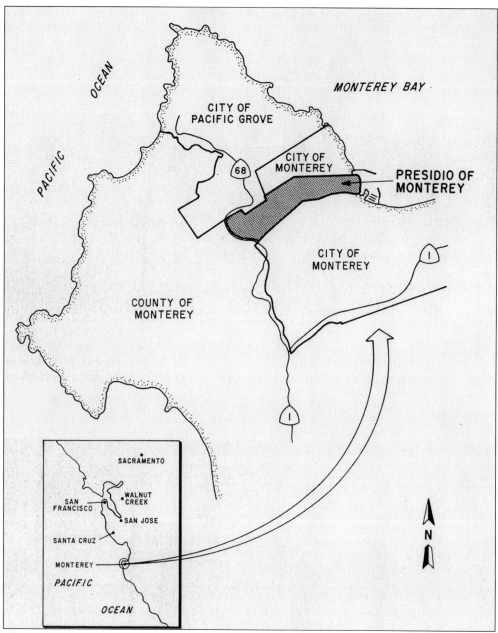

This map shows the regional location of the Presidio of Monterey on the central coast of California and on the Monterey Peninsula. The Presidio of Monterey, located about 125 miles south of San Francisco, consists of 392 acres of land.

African-American "Buffalo Soldiers" of the 1st Squadron, 9th U.S. Cavalry (Colored)—as the regiment was then called—were posted to the Monterey Military Reservation in the fall of 1902 after having participated in the Philippine Insurrection. This photo shows Buffalo Soldiers in about 1903 near their tent encampment near China Point in Pacific Grove, where the Hopkins Marine Station is now located.

Members of the 1st Squadron, 9th Cavalry—Buffalo Soldiers—after having received and broken in new horses, ride in a parade in Pacific Grove in about 1903.

This photograph of Monterey Bay, from the early 1900s, was taken from the old ramparts of Fort Mervine on the Presidio of Monterey.

This c. 1910 photograph was taken from the ruins of Fort Mervine facing uphill, away from Monterey Bay towards the west. The empty Soldier Field is on the right of the photograph, and eight barracks, completed by the 15th Infantry in 1903, appear in the center. The building on the far left was completed in 1904 and originally served as a gymnasium and post exchange facility.

This is a view from about 1910 over the Presidio of Monterey parade field, Soldier Field, facing east towards Monterey Bay. The eight barracks completed in 1903 are on the right, and

Local spectators, many in new and novel automobiles, watch soldiers parade on Soldier Field during the 1906 to 1909 period.

PARADE GROUNDS & BARRAC
PRESIDIO OF MONTEREY CA

the Officers Club, built in 1905, is on the left.

Historic artillery pieces, gun limbers, and stacked roundshot remained in the Fort Mervine area in the early 1900s.

This vintage postcard, from about 1908, shows Soldier Field with Monterey Bay in the background. This postcard, according to a small inscription, was "made exp. for 'Del Monte [Hotel] Curio Room.'"

In this *c.* 1910 view, spectators gather on benches to watch an event on Soldier Field. The eight barracks on the right were completed by the 15th Infantry in 1903.

Infantrymen stand at attention during a review held on Soldier Field in about 1910.

This is another view, from about 1910, of the barracks constructed in 1903. Each barracks (there were 12 built by the 15th Infantry in 1903) was designed to hold an infantry company, and included a porch or veranda that extended the length of the entire building. The barracks were long and narrow, usually one room deep, with many opposing windows for cross ventilation.

This 4,998-square-foot brick and frame building, now numbered Building 221, was completed in 1904 at a cost of $19,490. It originally served as the post exchange (including shoe shop and barber shop) and gymnasium. In 1938, this building became the headquarters of the 11th Cavalry Regiment, and over the years since has served as band barracks, post library and lecture hall, garrison headquarters, and Non-Commissioned Officers (NCO) Club. It is now an all-ranks social club.

Infantry soldiers march in formation near the post exchange in about 1910.

The 8,860-square-foot Officers Club, built overlooking Soldier Field at a cost of $5,599, was completed in 1905. It served as the center of the officers' social life, especially when troop units were stationed at the Presidio of Monterey prior to World War II. The Officers Club was closed in 1990.

Building 302 was constructed as the Post Hospital in 1905. It cost $19,839 to build, and consisted of 10,220 square feet of space. It later served as Post Headquarters and as the NCO Club in the 1950s until it became the Service Club in 1954, the year this photograph was taken. This building was torn down in 1978.

Soldiers of Company B, 20th Infantry Regiment, prepare for drill and ceremonies training in

Wearing dress uniforms, soldiers of Company D, 20th Infantry Regiment, pose on the steps of their barracks at the Presidio of Monterey for a unit photograph in 1907. Capt. Charles

this *c.* 1906 view. They stand in front of conical tents with Monterey Bay in the background.

Crawford was Company D commander at the time, and Lt. Truman W. Carrithers and 2nd Lt. Clifford C. Early were the other two officers in the company.

Soldiers of Company D, 20th Infantry Regiment pose in their field uniforms in front of their barracks at the Presidio of Monterey. An inscription on the back of this photograph, dated

This 1907 photograph shows a smaller group of soldiers of Company D, 20th Infantry

June 11, 1907, states, "Dear Father, I will send you this picture[;] it is my Co. Lay it up and keep it so if I ever get out I can see it."

Regiment, at the Presidio of Monterey. The two men in white on the left are probably cooks.

Soldiers of the 12th Infantry Regiment arrive at the Monterey Train Depot in this

The U.S. Army School of Musketry, the forerunner of the Infantry School, operated at the Presidio of Monterey from 1907 to 1913. This 1911 photograph shows the School of Musketry

c. 1909 photograph.

cadre, trainers, and students.

This was the rifle marksmanship range at the Presidio of Monterey, around 1906–1909. The range was located west of Rifle Range Road, where Combs Hall and Kendall Hall (Buildings 627 and 629 respectively) now stand.

This noncommissioned officer was the quartermaster sergeant of the 12th Infantry Regiment at the Presidio of Monterey during the period from 1909 to 1915.

Lt. Truman W. Carrithers, Company D, 20th Infantry, and a unit mascot pose in this photograph from about 1907.

Commodore John Drake Sloat commanded the U.S. Pacific Squadron and was responsible for the American capture of Monterey and annexation of California on July 7, 1846. To commemorate this historical occasion, the Sloat Monument was built on a bluff overlooking the eastern part of the post and Monterey Bay beyond. The cornerstone was laid in 1896, and the official dedication of the Sloat Monument, as shown in this photograph, took place on June 14, 1910.

This photograph shows the Sloat Monument after it was unveiled on June 14, 1910.

The 25-foot-tall Sloat Monument, capped by a granite eagle, is frequently the focal point of historical ceremonies, as it was in this 1965 photograph. The Coast Guard Wharf and Monterey Bay are in the background.

Lt. Joseph W. Stilwell, who was promoted to four-star general and commanded the China-Burma-India Theater in World War II, was assigned to the 12th Infantry Regiment at the

This photograph shows Quarters 357 as it appeared in 1999.

Presidio of Monterey in 1912–1913. This photograph is believed to be of Lieutenant Stilwell in front of Quarters 357 during that time.

A small plaque, as shown in this 1999 photograph, has been placed in front of Quarters 327, designating it the "Stilwell House."

The Presidio of Monterey's Artillery Street Gate is shown in this 1912 photograph. The Sloat Monument can be seen on the high ground to the guard's right.

The Artillery Street Gate was improved during the World War I era, as shown in this photograph. The large stone monument with the Gothic cross, seen on the left in this photograph, marks the spot near which Sebastian Vizcaino first came ashore and planted the Spanish flag on December 16, 1602. On May 31, 1770, Father Junipero Serra landed near this same site and met with the explorer Gaspar de Portola to re-claim Alta California for Spain.

The 12th Infantry Regiment established camp and conducted field training at Pebble Beach in 1912.

The 3rd Squadron, 1st Cavalry Regiment is shown here formed up for a parade on Soldier Field

on September 21, 1914.

The commander, staff, and band of the 12th Infantry Regiment prepare to march in formation at Soldier Field in about 1912. This photograph is the first of five panels that showed the entire

regiment in formation. The ramparts of old Fort Mervine and the Sloat Monument can be seen overlooking Monterey Bay to the right; two large oil tanks can barely be seen on the left.

Soldiers from the Presidio of Monterey conduct rifle marksmanship training on the sand dunes near the beach at Monterey Bay during World War I.

Two

1919–1946

THE CAVALRY ERA
AND WORLD WAR II

The 11th Cavalry Regiment was posted to the Presidio of Monterey from 1919 to 1940, and the 2nd Battalion, 76th Field Artillery Regiment (Horse), with its horse-drawn .75 mm howitzers, was stationed at the Presidio from 1922 to 1940. This photograph shows these units on parade at the Presidio in 1933, with the 11th Cavalry color guard in the foreground and elements of the 76th Field Artillery in the background.

The large oil tanks and plant of the Associated Oil Company, located between the Presidio of Monterey and Cannery Row, caught fire in September 1924, sending billowing black clouds of smoke into the air. This three-day fire endangered both the city and Presidio of Monterey.

Soldiers from the Presidio of Monterey helped fight the 1924 oil tank fire, and two soldiers—Pvt. George Bolio, of Headquarters Troop, 11th Cavalry, and Pvt. Eustace V. Watkins, of Battery E, 76th Field Artillery—were killed while fighting the fire. Private Bolio Road on the Presidio of Monterey is named after this soldier.

This photograph also shows Presidio of Monterey soldiers trying to extinguish the 1924 oil tank fire.

The horrific 1924 oil tank fire blackened the skies over the Presidio of Monterey and the surrounding area.

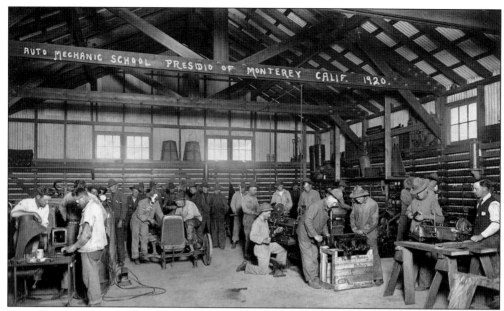

Even though the post–World War I units at the Presidio of Monterey depended on four-legged horsepower for mobility and to tow their artillery, trucks and other vehicles using the internal combustion engine could not be ignored. This 1920 photograph shows soldiers attending auto mechanic training at the Presidio of Monterey.

It took able musicians and skilled riders with well-trained horses to serve in the mounted 11th Cavalry band in 1920.

The 11th Cavalry rode down Lighthouse Avenue in Monterey while participating in the July 4th parade in 1930.

Officers of the 11th Cavalry lead the regiment in a parade on Alvarado Street in downtown Monterey in 1933.

New cavalrymen were taught to ride on a saddled barrel attached to ropes pulled by fellow soldiers to replicate the actions of a bucking horse.

Sergeant Sapash was a longtime soldier in the 11th Cavalry noted for his superb horse riding and training abilities. He is shown in this photograph with two fine cavalry mounts.

In this photograph, Sergeant Sapash is jumping his horse over an obstacle. Both rider and horse are in fine form.

Horsemanship training in the 11th Cavalry took many forms. It increased soldier riding proficiency and provided physical training, recreation, and enhanced unit esprit de corps. The 11th Cavalry also had a horsemanship gymkhana team that provided demonstrations. In this photograph, mounted cavalrymen form a five-man human pyramid while riding three horses.

In this photograph, the 11th Cavalry horsemanship gymkhana team demonstrates a mounted cavalryman jumping over the "human hurdle."

The cavalryman in this photograph jumps his horse through a large flaming hoop, a practice that encouraged boldness, courage, and teamwork in both soldier and mount.

The 11th Cavalry also had a mounted lance-armed silent drill team. Its members conducted various drills without verbal commands, and the team was also used for public relations purposes and demonstrations. This practice developed discipline and proficiency in both its human and equine members.

This photograph shows the 11th Cavalry silent drill team rehearsing at the Presidio of Monterey in the 1930s

Soldiers of the 11th Cavalry conduct mounted training on a Monterey Bay beach in the 1930s.

Cavalry troopers race down a large sand dune near 17 Mile Drive on the Monterey Peninsula in the 1930s.

The 11th Cavalry had a machine gun troop armed with Browning M1917A1 .30 caliber water-cooled machine guns. This was the standard machine gun of U.S. forces in World War I and was used extensively in World War II. In this *c.* 1930 photograph, cavalrymen conduct maintenance on their machine guns in front of unit barracks.

The field gear of an interwar 11th Cavalry trooper, including the equipment needed to take care of his horse, is depicted here laid out for inspection.

The motion picture *Sergeant Murphy*, starring a young Ronald Reagan as a cavalry private (left) and Mary Maguire, was filmed at the Presidio of Monterey in 1937. Soldiers of the 11th Cavalry served as extras in the movie. On the right is Lt. (later Maj. Gen.) Robert G. Fergusson, 11th Cavalry. Reagan later recalled, "We drove up the beautiful Monterey Peninsula, to the 11th Cavalry, where all the outdoor shooting would take place. This was a little more homelike and familiar to me than the sound stage at the studio." The title of the film refers to a horse.

A Great Dane named "Duke" was the mascot of F Troop, 11th Cavalry, at the Presidio of Monterey. This photograph of Duke was taken during the filming of *Sergeant Murphy* in 1937.

A lieutenant colonel of the 11th Cavalry congratulates First Sgt. C.E. Lewis (center) on his retirement from the Army in August 1934. The soldier on the right holds a set of silverware to be given to First Sergeant Lewis as a retirement gift from his fellow cavalrymen.

Soldier Field at the Presidio of Monterey was refurbished by Civilian Conservation Corps members in 1936 ("MCMXXXVI") by the addition of stone walls, cement bleachers,

Second Lt. (later Maj. Gen.) Perry B. Griffith, of the 11th Cavalry, and his wife, Florence, are shown in this 1937 photograph at the Presidio of Monterey.

and an entranceway and steps. Officers of the 11th Cavalry pose at Soldier Field in this 1937 photograph.

The officers and men of the 11th Cavalry prided themselves on their military prowess and expert horsemanship, and won many awards. In this 1934 photograph, an 11th Cavalry officer is holding the Marshall Cup awarded to the unit.

The 2nd Battalion, 76th Field Artillery Regiment (Horse), with its horse-drawn .75 mm howitzers, was stationed at the Presidio from 1922 to 1940. This 1925 photograph shows the

The 11th Cavalry horse show (exhibition) team won many awards in 1938, as shown in this photograph. The soldiers and horses in this photograph are, from left to right, (front row) Sergeant Sapash, Captain Thompson, Lieutenant Griffin, and Sergeant Neal; (back row) Private Durfee, "Prize," Captain Karr, "Snips," Captain Seeney, "Jay," Private Morgan, "Billy D.," Private Lorevele, "Charger," and Captain Marden. The horse and soldier to the far right in the second row are unidentified.

Headquarters Battery, 76th Field Artillery, on Soldier Field at the Presidio of Monterey.

One section of Battery E, 76th Field Artillery, is mounted and limbered up, prepared for action. This c. 1926 photograph does a superb job in showing the men, horses, and equipment in a two-gun towed .75 mm howitzer section.

The 76th Field Artillery also had its canine mascots in the 1930s. The dog and horse seemed to form an ideal partnership, as this gawking soldier looks away from the action.

The 76th Field Artillery conducted its live-fire artillery training at the Gigling Reservation, which was purchased by the War Department in 1917 and was later renamed Camp Ord, then Fort Ord. This 1920s photograph shows two soldiers in front of their pup tents during a field training exercise, with the horse picket lines to their rear.

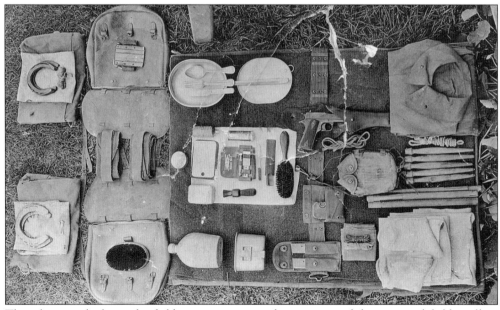

This photograph shows the field gear, weapon, and equipment of the mounted field artillery horse driver laid out for inspection in 1926.

Soldiers of Battery E, 76th Field Artillery stand in the chow line during a field training exercise in the Big Sur area in 1926.

A gun team of the 76th Field Artillery is on the march during an exercise near King City, California, in 1932.

This trooper and his mount take a break during the 76th Field Artillery's march to King City in 1932.

This 76th Field Artillery gun crew is at full gallop during an exercise at Camp Ord during the late 1930s. It was experienced Army horse riders and drivers from the 76th Field Artillery like these who drove the 300 chariots of the Pharaoh's Army during the 1923 filming of Cecil B. DeMille's epic movie *The Ten Commandments*. This movie was shot at Guadalupe on the central coast of California.

During a live-fire exercise at Gigling Reservation in the 1920s, this 76th Field Artillery gun crew takes a break. The soldiers are, from left to right, Sergeant Shaw, section chief; Corporal Tome, gunner; and Privates Morrison, Volpe, Miller, Biggs, and Johnson.

Soldiers in a field artillery unit's observation post played an integral part in the effective firing of the unit's guns. These soldiers observed the impact of the rounds, then adjusted them closer to the intended target. This is the 76th Field Artillery's observation post in action during a unit live-fire exercise at the Gigling Reservation in the 1920s.

When soldiers went to the field to train, the kitchen went with them to prepare their food. This photograph from the 1920s shows the mobile field kitchen of one battery of the 76th Field Artillery at the Gigling Reservation. Sergeant Campbell, with ladle in hand, is on the left of this picture, and Cook Spencer is on the right.

Posing proudly on his mount in this 1933 photograph is 2nd Lt. Bernard Thielen, a battery officer of the 76th Field Artillery at the Presidio of Monterey.

The stable area on the lower Presidio of Monterey is shown in this 1930s photograph. Monterey Bay is in the background.

The horse picket line in the stable area on the lower Presidio of Monterey is shown in this 1938 photograph. The Sloat Monument can be seen on the high ground in the center of this photo.

This is the wagon shed of the 76th Field Artillery, located near the stables on the lower Presidio of Monterey, in the 1930s.

E Troop, 11th Calvary.

This is the mess hall (dining facility) of E Troop, 11th Cavalry at the Presidio of Monterey, decorated for Thanksgiving dinner, 1934.

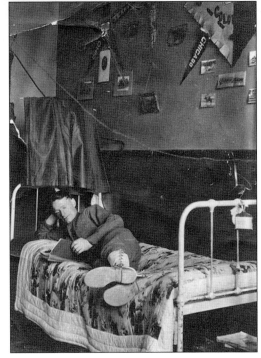

As shown in this 1920s photograph, the living accommodations for a private soldier in the barracks were more comfortable than one may imagine. This reading and relaxing trooper was in the 11th Cavalry.

From time immemorial, soldiers living in barracks have passed the time engaging in card games and other relatively harmless activities. This 1924 photograph shows 11th Cavalry troopers playing poker in the barracks.

These two disciplined 11th Cavalry troopers pose on the porch of their barracks after conducting a drill with the "Patton" model cavalry sword.

The 11th Cavalry, like many other Army units, conducted competitive team sports to increase soldier physical fitness, build teamwork, and increase unit esprit de corps. The F Troop baseball team was the Presidio of Monterey champion in 1934. The soldiers shown in this photograph are, from left to right, (front row) Due, McKinley, Gayne, Kemp, and Larson; (back row) Nelson, Paul, Thompson, Smith, and Parent.

The F Troop, 11th Cavalry team was the Presidio of Monterey basketball champion in 1935. Team members shown in this photograph are, from left to right, (front row) Lieutenant Vars, Frocbraug, Thompson, Kemp, and Smith; (back row) Sildicka, Oswald, Nelson, Due, and Parent.

The 76th Field Artillery also had a baseball team at the Presidio of Monterey in the 1930s, although it does not seem to have won as many games as its cavalry counterparts. Nicknamed the "Bloomer Girls," this team consisted of, from left to right, (front row) Perry, Mays, Regan, Hughes, and Norwood; (back row) Hutton, Harlin, McAndrews, Mattingly, Daily, and Palmer. From their appearances, it seems the artillerymen did not take the game of baseball too seriously!

The 11th Cavalry sponsored and conducted the regional Citizens' Military Training Corps (CMTC) summer camps in the 1920s and 1930s, and Reserve Officer Training Corps (ROTC) summer camps in the 1930s, at both the Presidio of Monterey and nearby Camp Del Monte. This photograph shows ROTC cadets conducting physical training at the Presidio of Monterey in the 1930s.

These two relaxed cadets in their fatigue uniforms attended ROTC summer camp at the Presidio of Monterey in 1938.

Presenting a more martial appearance in their dress uniforms, Cadets Robert Coffin (left) and Wendell Best (right) also attended ROTC summer in 1938 at the Presidio of Monterey.

Cadet Dave Boles wears a gas mask during training at the Presidio of Monterey ROTC summer camp in 1939.

Camp Del Monte was a temporary summer camp established each year, beginning in about 1922, on the spacious grounds of the Del Monte Hotel (now the Naval Postgraduate School). It was renamed Camp John Pryor, in honor of a local resident who had won the Distinguished Service Cross in World War I, in 1930, and moved to the Presidio of Monterey in 1932. This photograph shows cadets of CMTC Company B marching at the Presidio of Monterey in the 1930s.

CMTC cadets also conducted their rifle marksmanship training at the Presidio of Monterey in the 1930s.

CMTC cadets from the Presidio of Monterey trained in horsemanship and cavalry tactics at the Gigling Reservation in about 1930.

These men attended the CMTC training at the Presidio of Monterey in 1933. They are, from left to right, unknown, Presley, Clough, Albert Miller, John Longly, and Myers.

Building 228 was constructed on the Presidio of Monterey in 1934 to serve as the gymnasium and post exchange. It was then called the Presidio Recreation Center.

A swimming pool (designated Building 227) was built in the back of the Presidio Recreation Center. It was used frequently by soldiers, as shown in this 1938 photograph.

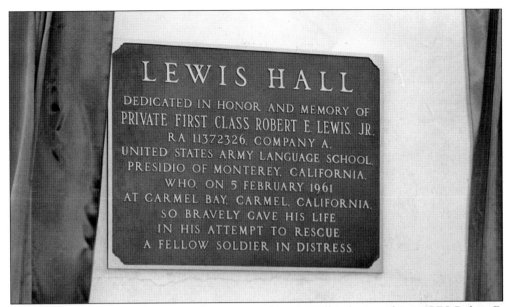

The Presidio Recreation Center was later renamed Lewis Hall in honor of Army PFC Robert E. Lewis Jr. While a student at the Army Language School in 1961, Lewis drowned while trying to rescue a fellow soldier who was drowning in nearby Carmel Bay.

A renovated Lewis Hall now serves as the Outdoor Recreation Center for the Presidio of Monterey.

Building 208 was constructed of concrete in 1910 at a cost of $15,685. Its original purpose was to serve as an assembly hall, but it later became the post theater, a function it still serves to this day. The large wooden entrance doors in the center were hand-carved in 1935. A porch-like façade was added in 1936, mainly to provide overhead cover to waiting patrons.

The large mahogany doors of Building 208 were hand-carved by Carlos Ayala, an Aztec Indian from Mexico. They were completed in 1935 as part of a Works Project Administration (WPA) project for Monterey Peninsula artists during the Depression. Ayala was reportedly a direct descendent of the woodcarver to Montezuma, the last Aztec ruler of Mexico.

The interior of Building 208 was completely renovated in 1934 to 1935. One contemporary source stated that before the renovation, the interior of the theater was "cheerless and barn-like," with the seats being a mixture of barracks chairs, mess hall stools, and backless benches. As shown in this photograph (facing the rear of the theater), new seats were installed, coats of arms of Army units that had served at the Presidio of Monterey were painted on the walls, and the front of the balcony was decorated in lemon gold with orange California poppies.

William Kneass of Carmel carved a six-foot pine eagle that was covered in gold leaf (shown in this photograph) and installed at the archway of the stage in the post theater in 1936, adding an additional touch of class.

This is a World War II–era aerial photograph of the Presidio of Monterey. Stables and warehouses are located in the foreground, and the arrowhead-shaped ramparts of Fort Mervine can be seen in the left center of the photograph. Near the top left corner of this photograph are a number of barracks and administrative buildings that were built on Soldier Field at the beginning of World War II and served as the reception station. The buildings on Soldier Field were torn down in about 1974. Monterey Bay and moored boats are in the lower right corner.

The III Corps Headquarters was located at the Presidio of Monterey during World War II. This 1944 photograph shows personnel from the III Corps G-2 (Intelligence) section, with members of the 203rd Counter-Intelligence Battalion.

In 1945, the Presidio of Monterey served as a Civil Affairs Staging and Holding Area (CASA) for civil affairs soldiers preparing for duty with the occupation forces in Japan. This photograph includes three soldiers assigned to a civil affairs unit at the Presidio of Monterey. They are, from left to right, Staff Sgt James Carter Jr.; Sgt. Owen B. Prevost (off duty in civilian clothes); and Staff Sgt. Paul F. Shafer.

SERGEANT TIPPY

1931-1943

Old Timer, man had no better friend!
Words fail, when thinking of your end;
Your welcome bark, and that "dry run;"
Yes, old fellow, we sure had fun.
That grand spirit and fighting heart;
It was a tank that made us part.

You were getting old and lame,
But even "Horse" couldn't make you tame:
For a dog, you were super super
Not a beggar, but a real trooper.
How you'd sit still when told, "stay there"!
Wouldn't move a muscle or a hair.

We gave you a funeral, a handsome one,
It was the least we could have done;
The "old 11th" honours you this day,
Killed in service of the U.S.A.!
Only one time did you make a slip,
A.W.O.L., Dear Old Tip.

Beside your grave "Taps" was blown;
A better soldier, we've never known;
In your own bed-roll, you lie at rest,
A shelter-half covers your chest;
And though no longer your tail can wag,
We salute you as we would the Flag!

Your Buddies

"Sergeant Tippy" was a mascot of the 11th Cavalry while stationed at the Presidio of Monterey. When he died in 1943, Sergeant Tippy was given a soldier's funeral and memorialized by his "buddies."

86

Three
1947–1963
THE ARMY LANGUAGE SCHOOL

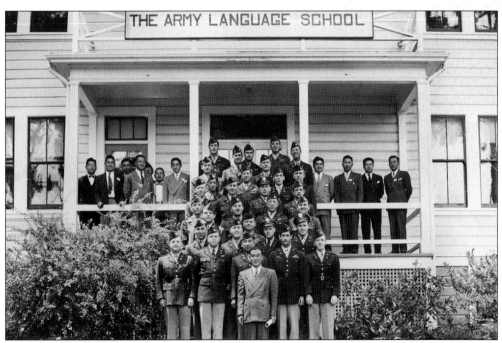

In 1946, after World War II, the Military Intelligence Service Language School (MISLS) was moved from Minnesota to the Presidio of Monterey. It added Russian, Chinese, Korean, Arabic, and six other languages to its curriculum and was renamed the Army Language School (ALS) in 1947. This photograph shows the ALS instructors at the Presidio of Monterey in 1948.

The forerunner of the Army Language School was the Fourth U.S. Army Intelligence School, established in an old hangar at Crissy Field on the Presidio of San Francisco on November 1, 1941. The school's mission was to teach Japanese to second-generation Japanese-American (Nisei) soldiers to use in a possible war with Japan. On May 25, 1942, the school was moved to Camp Savage, Minnesota, and was renamed the Military Intelligence Service Language School. This was the headquarters of the MISLS at Camp Savage in 1942.

This view shows the MISLS instructors' office at Camp Savage from 1942 to 1944.

MISLS students are shown in this c. 1942 photograph being issued Japanese language class textbooks at the school supply room at Camp Savage.

In this photograph from about 1942, Instructor Shoji Takimoto is shown teaching a class in Japanese small-unit tactics at the MISLS at Camp Savage.

This building served as an MISLS classroom at Camp Savage between 1942 and 1944.

Soldier students diligently study their Japanese at the MISLS, Camp Savage, during the 1942–1944 period.

Col. Kai E. Rasmussen (left) congratulates a student after completing the rigorous MISLS course during World War II. Rasmussen became the commandant of the MISLS at Camp Savage in June 1942, and moved the MISLS to Fort Snelling, Minnesota in 1944, and to the Presidio of Monterey in 1946.

The MISLS moved from Camp Savage, to Fort Snelling, Minnesota, on August 15, 1944. This photograph shows students studying in an MISLS classroom at Fort Snelling in 1944.

This photograph, taken after the MISLS had moved from Fort Snelling to the Presidio of Monterey in 1946, shows Col. Elliott R. Thorpe (right) presenting War Department awards for their superb wartime MISLS instructor service to, from left to right, Yutaka Munakata, Tom Tanimoto, Tetsue Imagawa, and Shigeya Kihara. Colonel Thorpe succeeded Colonel Rasmussen in command of the MISLS in July 1946

The MISLS was renamed the Army Language School (ALS) in 1947. In this late 1940s photograph, Japanese language instructor Tetsue Imagawa provides an overview of language training equipment.

ALS instructor Capt. Donald Likas (standing) teaches Greek to his students in 1947.

Alternate methods and reinforcement of foreign language learning took place in many scenarios at the ALS. In this late 1940s photograph, the ALS Russian Choir, consisting of Russian language students singing Russian songs, presents a concert. The Russian Choir was considered excellent and even made a few records.

These are instructors in the ALS Japanese Department in the early 1950s.

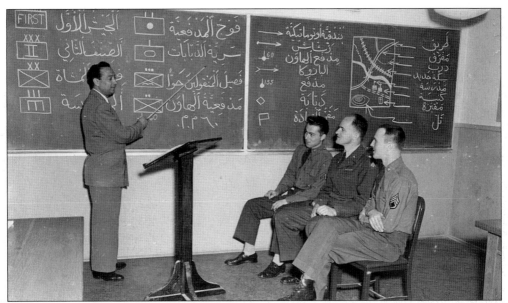

Kamil T. Said (standing), head of the ALS Arabic Language Department, teaches Arabic military terminology to students, from left to right, PFC Henry Lutz, Lt. Col. Donald D. Dunlop, and Staff Sgt. Donald R. Wyatt, on April 17, 1952.

Robert B. Franco, instructor in the ALS Spanish Language Department, conducts a class on April 17, 1952, at a terrain model of a small village, using Spanish vocabulary that identified the characteristics of the city and of the countryside. The students are, from left to right, Col. H.A. Welsch, Master Sgt. Myron J. Donnelly, Capt. Robert K. Douglas, and Corp. Robert A. Fitzpatrick.

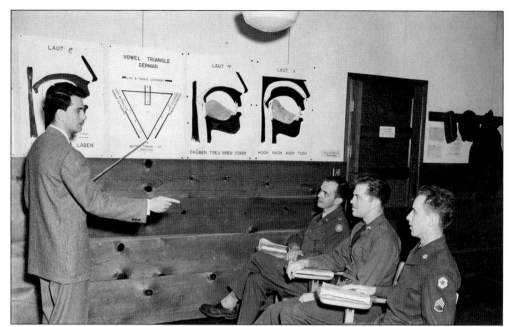

Chairman of the ALS German Language Department Klaus A. Mueller (standing) drills a class in German pronunciation with the aid of wall charts on April 18, 1952. His students are, from left to right, Lt. Col. Martin B. Chandler, Pvt. William C. Starkweather, and Sgt. Charles L. Bryan.

Records are being cut for the use of ALS students in this April 17, 1952 photograph. Those working in the Sound Recording Studio are, from left to right, Sgt. William G. Young, Thomas Ozamoto, and PFC Ben Hoshina.

ALS students, from left to right, Sgt. First Class John T. Krulikoski, Lt. C.R. Lockhard, Sgt. First Class J.A. Lana, and Capt. L.B. Pydeski rehearse in traditional costume "The Krakowiak," a famous Polish folk dance for the April 25, 1952 ALS Festival.

The Presidio Recreation Center (later renamed Lewis Hall) is decorated for the ALS Festival on April 25, 1952.

This ALS student (center) is being taught Japanese customs, traditions, and the vernacular Japanese language in this photograph from the early 1950s.

Instructors of the ALS Chinese Mandarin Department pose in front of a classroom at the Presidio of Monterey in 1954.

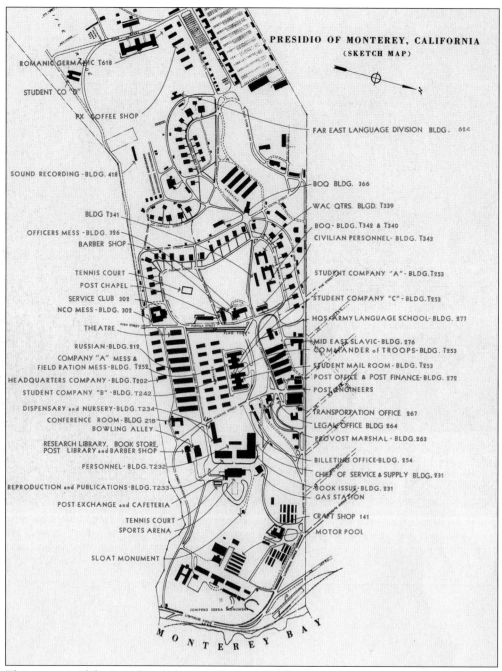

This is a map of the Presidio of Monterey from about 1958.

This c. 1962 aerial photograph of the Presidio of Monterey was taken from over the Monterey Bay facing west. In this photograph, the stables that were situated on the "lower" Presidio of Monterey, close to the Bay, no longer exist. In addition, temporary World War II buildings continue to occupy Soldier Field. The orientation of this aerial photograph is almost identical to that of the map on the preceding page.

A staff officer (standing) briefs Col. Walter E. Krause, ALS commandant from 1954 to 1959, on possible plans for future development of the facilities at the Presidio of Monterey.

Four

1963–2003

THE DEFENSE LANGUAGE INSTITUTE
FOREIGN LANGUAGE CENTER

Viewed from near the Artillery Street Gate in the early 1960s, Fisherman's Wharf and the
marina in Monterey Bay are situated basically at the foot of the Presidio of Monterey.

Col. Kai E. Rasmussen (fourth from right), commandant of the Military Intelligence Service Language School (MISLS) from 1942 to 1946, is shown visiting "old hands," MISLS Japanese language instructors who continued to serve as language instructors in the Far East Division at the Defense Language Institute, West Coast Branch (as the Army Language School was renamed in 1963), November 16, 1966. The men in this photograph are, from left to right, Paul Tekawa, Shoj Takimoto, John Hamamura, Goro Yamamoto, Akira Oshida, Colonel Rasmussen, Kaoru Tsukimura, Tetsuo Imagawa, and George Sakai.

After the Defense Department consolidated much of its foreign language training in 1963 and redesignated the Army Language School at the Presidio of Monterey the Defense Language Institute, West Coast Branch (DLIWC), plans were made to expand the school's facilities and infrastructure. In this May 29, 1963 photograph, Maj. Gen. Edwin H.J. Carns (center), Fort Ord's commanding general, is shown wielding the shovel in a groundbreaking ceremony for a new student barracks at the Presidio of Monterey. Others in this photograph are, from left to right, Col. Chester M. Stratton, Fort Ord logistics officer; Col. Richard J. Long, commandant, DLIWC; General Carns; Lt. Col. Leslie B. Enoch, Presidio of Monterey Deputy Post Commander; and Fred R. Fader, project engineer for the Corps of Engineers, Sacramento District, Monterey Office.

Building 113 (at right), constructed of wood and corrugated metal in 1921 for $9,110, was originally built as a quartermaster workshop. After serving a number of purposes, it was converted to the Presidio of Monterey Museum in 1967. The Sloat Monument is on the high ground in the center of the photograph.

This photograph shows Building 113 and the surrounding area after it was converted to the Presidio of Monterey Museum in 1967.

To permit the construction of new permanent buildings for language training, six wooden structures located near the old upper cavalry drill field (near the rifle range), shown in this photograph, were demolished in June 1966.

The first permanent building for language training purposes was the Western and Southern European Division (WASED) Building, Building 620. This photograph shows construction progress on the WASED Building on February 4, 1964.

This photograph shows the WASED Building in August 1966 after completion. Building 620 was later renamed Nisei Hall and dedicated to the Japanese-American soldiers who served as U.S. Army military linguists during World War II.

DLIWC language students study in a then state-of-the-art language laboratory in the WASED Building in about 1966.

The former Officers Club was redesignated the International Language and Culture Center later in 1990 by Col. Donald C. Fischer Jr., commandant of the Defense Language Institute Foreign Language Center (DLIFLC, as the DLIWC was renamed in 1976). On January 21, 1993, it was renamed the Weckerling Center, in honor of Brig. Gen. John Weckerling, U.S. Army (Ret.), the "founder" of the MISLS in 1941.

The Presidio of Monterey Officers Club, Building 326, was constructed in 1905 and closed in 1990.

This is an aerial view of the Presidio of Monterey from the early 1980s, showing, in the top half of the photograph, the construction of permanent barracks and classroom buildings and expansion of the DLIFLC.

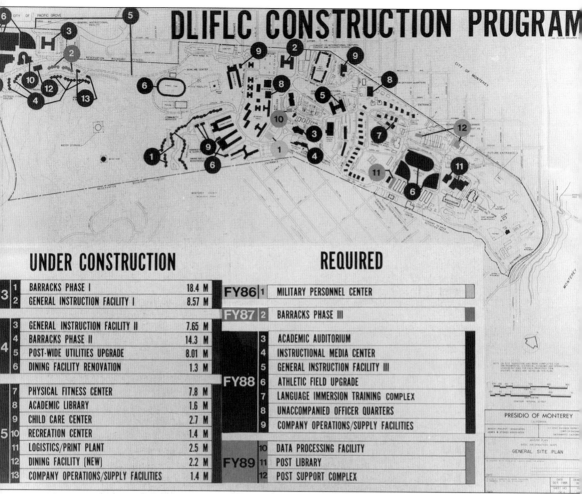

DLIFLC CONSTRUCTION PROGRAM

UNDER CONSTRUCTION			REQUIRED		
3	1	BARRACKS PHASE I	18.4 M	FY86	1	MILITARY PERSONNEL CENTER
	2	GENERAL INSTRUCTION FACILITY I	8.57 M			
				FY87	2	BARRACKS PHASE III
	3	GENERAL INSTRUCTION FACILITY II	7.65 M		3	ACADEMIC AUDITORIUM
4	4	BARRACKS PHASE II	14.3 M		4	INSTRUCTIONAL MEDIA CENTER
	5	POST-WIDE UTILITIES UPGRADE	8.01 M		5	GENERAL INSTRUCTION FACILITY III
	6	DINING FACILITY RENOVATION	1.3 M	FY88	6	ATHLETIC FIELD UPGRADE
	7	PHYSICAL FITNESS CENTER	7.8 M		7	LANGUAGE IMMERSION TRAINING COMPLEX
	8	ACADEMIC LIBRARY	1.6 M		8	UNACCOMPANIED OFFICER QUARTERS
	9	CHILD CARE CENTER	2.7 M		9	COMPANY OPERATIONS/SUPPLY FACILITIES
5	10	RECREATION CENTER	1.4 M		10	DATA PROCESSING FACILITY
	11	LOGISTICS/PRINT PLANT	2.5 M	FY89	11	POST LIBRARY
	12	DINING FACILITY (NEW)	2.2 M		12	POST SUPPORT COMPLEX
	13	COMPANY OPERATIONS/SUPPLY FACILITIES	1.4 M			

The 1980s was a period of tremendous expansion for the U.S. Army, as well as for language training and the DLIFLC. This map shows the "DLIFLC Construction Program" for fiscal year (FY) 1983 through FY 1989.

114

The "Russian Village" area of the DLIFLC, where Russian language students live in barracks, eat in a dining facility, and are taught in the Russian II School, is shown under construction in this 1985 aerial photograph.

This 14,000-pound aircraft carrier anchor is emplaced in front of and readily identifies Building 629, then housing the Naval Security Group, Detachment Monterey, in 1987.

NAKAMURA HALL

BUILDING 619 IS DEDICATED TO THE MEMORY OF
SERGEANT GEORGE ICHIRO NAKAMURA
1923 – 1945

WHO DIED AS A RESULT OF WOUNDS RECEIVED IN ACTION
29 JUNE 1945 IN THE PHILIPPINE ISLANDS. THE SILVER STAR WA
AWARDED POSTHUMOUSLY TO SERGEANT NAKAMURA FOR HIS ACTIONS
THAT DAY. SERGEANT NAKAMURA GRADUATED FROM THE MILITARY
INTELLIGENCE SERVICE LANGUAGE SCHOOL, IN MINNESOTA, IN 1944

HACHIYA HALL

BUILDING 621 IS DEDICATED TO THE MEMORY OF
TECHNICIAN THIRD CLASS FRANK TADAKAZU HACHIYA
1920 – 1944

WHO DIED AS A RESULT OF WOUNDS RECEIVED IN ACTION
30 DECEMBER 1944 IN THE PHILIPPINE ISLANDS. THE SILVER ST
WAS AWARDED POSTHUMOUSLY TO TECHNICIAN THIRD CLASS HACHIY
FOR HIS ACTIONS THAT DAY. TECHNICIAN THIRD CLASS HACHIYA
GRADUATED FROM THE MILITARY INTELLIGENCE SERVICE LANGUAG
SCHOOL, IN MINNESOTA, IN 1943.

MIZUTARI HALL

BUILDING 623 IS DEDICATED TO THE MEMORY OF
TECHNICAL SERGEANT YUKITAKA "TERRY" MIZUTARI
1920 – 1944

WHO DIED AS A RESULT OF WOUNDS RECEIVED IN ACTION 23 JUN
1944 IN NEW GUINEA. THE SILVER STAR WAS AWARDED POSTHUMOUSI
TO TECHNICAL SERGEANT YUKITAKA MIZUTARI FOR HIS ACTIONS TH
DAY. TECHNICAL SERGEANT MIZUTARI GRADUATED FROM THE MILITA
INTELLIGENCE SERVICE LANGUAGE SCHOOL, IN MINNESOTA, IN 194

Adjacent DLIFLC classroom Buildings 619, 621, and 623 were constructed in 1975. Each was named for an MISLS graduate who was killed in action and recognized for his gallantry during World War II. These graduates were Sgt. George I. Nakamura (Building 619), Tech. Third Class Frank T. Hachiya (Building 621), and Tech. Sgt. Yukitaki Mizutari (Building 623).

Sgt. George I. Nakamura, born in 1923, graduated from the MISLS in 1944. He was killed in action in the Philippines on June 29, 1945, and awarded the Silver Star posthumously for his gallantry in action. Building 619, with a 98-person auditorium, 31 classrooms, and 2 language laboratories, is named Nakamura Hall in his honor.

A 1943 graduate of the MISLS, Tech. Third Class Frank T. Hachiya was born in 1920 and died of wounds received in combat in the Philippines on December 30, 1944. He received the Silver Star posthumously for his bravery. The 56-classroom Building 621 was dedicated as Hachiya Hall.

Born in 1920 and a 1943 MISLS graduate, Tech. Sergeant Yukitaka Mizutari was killed in action in New Guinea on 23 June 1944 and received the Silver Star for his intrepidity in action. Building 623, with 44 classrooms, was named Mizutari Hall in his memory.

Building 610, with 86 classrooms and 6 language laboratories, was completed in 1984 at a cost of $6 million. It was named Munakata Hall in honor of Yutaka Munakata, one of the first four MISLS language instructors who served at the MISLS and its successor organizations from 1942 to 1981. He later served as WASED director and retired as an assistant dean.

Yutaka Munakata, who served as an Army language instructor for almost four decades, is the namesake of Munakata Hall.

Building 614, completed in 1977, is the headquarters building of the DLIFLC. It was named in honor of Col. Kai E. Rasmussen, MISLS commandant from 1942 to 1946.

RASMUSSEN HALL
DEDICATED TO THE MEMORY OF
COLONEL KAI EDUARD RASMUSSEN
1902 – 1988

RASMUSSEN WAS THE FIRST COMMANDANT OF THE MILITARY INTELLIGENCE SERVICE LANGUAGE SCHOOL (MISLS), PREDECESSOR OF THE DEFENSE LANGUAGE INSTITUTE. BORN IN 1902 IN HELSINGE, DENMARK, HE EMIGRATED TO THE UNITED STATES IN 1922 AND ENLISTED IN THE UNITED STATES ARMY. HE GRADUATED FROM THE UNITED STATES MILITARY ACADEMY IN 1929 AS A COAST ARTILLERY OFFICER AND FROM 1936 TO 1940 HE SERVED AS A MILITARY ATTACHE IN IMPERIAL JAPAN. IN 1941 CAPTAIN RASMUSSEN AND MAJOR JOHN WECKERLING ESTABLISHED THE SECRET JAPANESE LANGUAGE SCHOOL AT THE PRESIDIO OF SAN FRANCISCO WITH SIXTY STUDENTS. WHEN WAR BROKE OUT HE ROSE TO THE RANK OF COLONEL AND HEADED MISLS AS IT MOVED TO CAMP SAVAGE (1942-44) AND LATER FORT SNELLING (1944-46), MINNESOTA, UNTIL IT CAME TO THE PRESIDIO OF MONTEREY IN 1946. THE SCHOOL'S 6,000 GRADUATES SERVED THROUGHOUT THE PACIFIC THEATRE DURING THE WAR AND THE OCCUPATION OF JAPAN THAT FOLLOWED. HE EARNED THE DEVOTION OF HIS PREDOMINANTLY JAPANESE-AMERICAN STUDENTS AND STAFF BY PLACING GREAT FAITH IN THEIR LOYALTY AND ABILITIES AND WAS AWARDED THE LEGION OF MERIT FOR HIS DEDICATED LEADERSHIP. HE SUBSEQUENTLY SERVED AS MILITARY ATTACHE TO NORWAY AND ON GENERAL MacARTHUR'S INTELLIGENCE STAFF DURING THE KOREAN WAR, BEFORE HIS RETIREMENT IN 1955.

This is the commemorative plaque on Rasmussen Hall, which was dedicated to Colonel Rasmussen in 1988.

AISO LIBRARY
DEDICATED TO THE MEMORY OF
JUDGE JOHN FUJIO AISO
1909 – 1987

AISO WAS THE FIRST DIRECTOR OF ACADEMIC TRAINING OF THE MILITARY
INTELLIGENCE SERVICE LANGUAGE SCHOOL (MISLS), PREDECESSOR OF
THE DEFENSE LANGUAGE INSTITUTE. HE WAS BORN IN 1909 IN BURBANK,
CALIFORNIA, THE SON OF JAPANESE IMMIGRANTS AND GRADUATED
FROM BROWN UNIVERSITY AND HARVARD LAW SCHOOL. IN 1936-37 HE
STUDIED AT CHUO UNIVERSITY, TOKYO, AND WORKED UNTIL 1941 FOR
A BRITISH COMPANY IN JAPANESE-OCCUPIED MANCHURIA. HE RETURNED
TO THE UNITED STATES IN EARLY 1941 AND WAS CONSCRIPTED INTO
THE ARMY. WITHIN MONTHS HE WAS RELEASED FROM ACTIVE DUTY
TO SERVE AS CHIEF INSTRUCTOR FOR THE HASTILY-FORMED SECRET
JAPANESE LANGUAGE SCHOOL. UNDER HIS INSPIRING LEADERSHIP AS
DIRECTOR OF ACADEMIC TRAINING, MISLS RAPIDLY EXPANDED. HE RECRUITED
INSTRUCTORS AND TRAINED THEM, DEVELOPED COURSE MATERIALS,
AND SET THE HIGHEST ACADEMIC STANDARDS. THE MORE THAN 6,000
MISLS GRADUATES CONTRIBUTED IMMEASURABLY TO THE AMERICAN
VICTORY OVER IMPERIAL JAPAN AND TO WINNING THE PEACE THAT
FOLLOWED. IN 1946 HE WAS GIVEN A DIRECT COMMISSION AS MAJOR
AND AWARDED THE LEGION OF MERIT. IN 1947 HE RESUMED THE
PRACTICE OF LAW IN LOS ANGELES, AND IN 1953 HE BECAME THE
FIRST JAPANESE-AMERICAN TO ENTER THE CALIFORNIA STATE JUDICIARY.
IN 1984 THE EMPEROR OF JAPAN AWARDED HIM THE 3RD CLASS ORDER
OF THE RISING SUN FOR HIS CONTRIBUTIONS TO UNDERSTANDING
AND FRIENDSHIP BETWEEN THE UNITED STATES AND JAPAN.

Completed in 1986, Building 617 is named the Aiso Library in honor of John F. Aiso, the first head instructor of the MISLS from 1941 to 1945. His later prominent career culminated in a judgeship.

Aiso Library was dedicated in honor of John F. Aiso in 1988, and his contributions to the MISLS and distinguished career are highlighted on this commemorative plaque.

On April 18, 1988, the Presidio of
Monterey hosted a ceremony to
commemorate the epic April 18, 1942
Doolittle bombing raid over Tokyo and to
honor the "Doolittle Raiders" who
participated in it. The guest of honor was
Monterey resident and the leader of the
"raid," retired U.S. Air Force General
James "Jimmy" H. Doolittle. General
Doolittle is shown at the podium in the
center of this photograph acknowledging
the applause of the audience at the
ceremony. Others in this photograph are,
from left to right, Brig. Gen. James
"Jimmy" Stewart, U.S. Air Force Reserve
(Retired) and eminent actor; the
superintendent of the Naval Postgraduate
School; General Doolittle; Maj. Gen.
Edwin H. Burba, Commanding Gen., 7th
Infantry Division (Light) and Fort Ord;
and Congressman Leon Panetta.

Gen. Jimmy Doolittle appears at the April
18, 1988 Presidio of Monterey ceremony
honoring him and the "Doolittle Raiders."

121

Col. Donald C. Fischer Jr., DLIFLC commandant, presides at a 1991 ceremony commemorating the 50th anniversary of the founding of the MISLS, the forerunner of the ALS and of the DLIFLC.

Former and current language instructors, including Ben de la Selva (pointing, right), view a mural commemorating the Middle East School during the DLIFLC's 1991 50th anniversary ceremony.

In 1994, with the closure of Fort Ord, the U.S. Army Garrison, Presidio of Monterey was established as a separate unit under the U.S. Army Training and Doctrine Command. Participating in the 1994 ceremony in which the new Garrison colors were unfurled is Col. Vladimir Sobichevsky (right), DLIFLC commandant.

On March 21, 1996, the DLIFLC's Troop Command was inactivated and officially redesignated the 229th Military Intelligence Battalion. In this photograph taken at the 1996 Soldier Field ceremony, Lt. Col. Jack Dees (left, back to camera), assisted by Command Sgt. Maj. Marvin Cobb (center) unfurl the new unit's colors.

U.S. Army Chief of Staff Gen. Eric K. Shinseki awarded a long-overdue Presidential Unit Citation to the Military Intelligence Service (MIS) in 2001 for "outstanding performance of duty in action against enemies of the United States from 1 May 1942 to 2 September 1945." In a 2001 ceremony at the Presidio of Monterey's Soldier Field, Col. Kevin M. Rice, DLIFLC commandant (in uniform), assisted by Shigeya Kihara (right), one of the first MISLS instructors, affix the Presidential Unit Citation to the DLIFLC's colors.

Many World War II Military Intelligence Service veterans participated in the 2001 Presidio of Monterey ceremony in which the MIS was awarded the Presidential Unit Citation.

In 2003, language training at the DLIFLC continued to expand and support national defense and the global war on terrorism. In this June 25, 2003 photograph, Navy Petty Officer First Class Martin Boese, a Persian-Farsi Military Language Instructor, teaches his basic Persian-Farsi course students in European School II, DLIFLC.

Each year, the DLIFLC hosts "Language Day," an event open to the public where language students demonstrate their language skills and departments show their course offerings to potential students. This photograph is from the DLIFLC Language Day 2002 at the Presidio of Monterey.

Turkish language students perform a traditional Turkish dance at the DLIFLC Language Day 2001.

Chinese language students man and parade the traditional Chinese dragon at the DLIFLC Language Day 2001.

Hyung C. Ko, assistant professor in the Korean Department, Asian School II, DLIFLC, encourages his students as they practice their basic Korean course language lesson, 2003.

DLIFLC language students access various computer programs to enhance their foreign language straining, 2003.

Asst. Prof. Ilya Levit, Russian Department A, European School II, DLIFLC, monitors his basic Russian course students in a language laboratory, 2003.

Col. Michael R. Simone (left), DLIFLC commandant, presents the Army Achievement Medal to Airman First Class Anna S. Sawyer, who graduated from the Chinese-Mandarin Course on both the Commandant's and the Provost's List, July 17, 2003. Airman Sawyer also earned First Place in the California State Chinese-Mandarin Speech Contest, and represented the United States at an international language competition in Beijing, China.